The Suebi: The History and Legacy of the Ancient Germanic Groups

By Charles River Editors

A Suebi vessel

About Charles River Editors

Charles River Editors is a boutique digital publishing company, specializing in bringing history back to life with educational and engaging books on a wide range of topics. Keep up to date with our new and free offerings with this 5 second sign up on our weekly mailing list, and visit Our Kindle Author Page to see other recently published Kindle titles.

We make these books for you and always want to know our readers' opinions, so we encourage you to leave reviews and look forward to publishing new and exciting titles each week.

Introduction

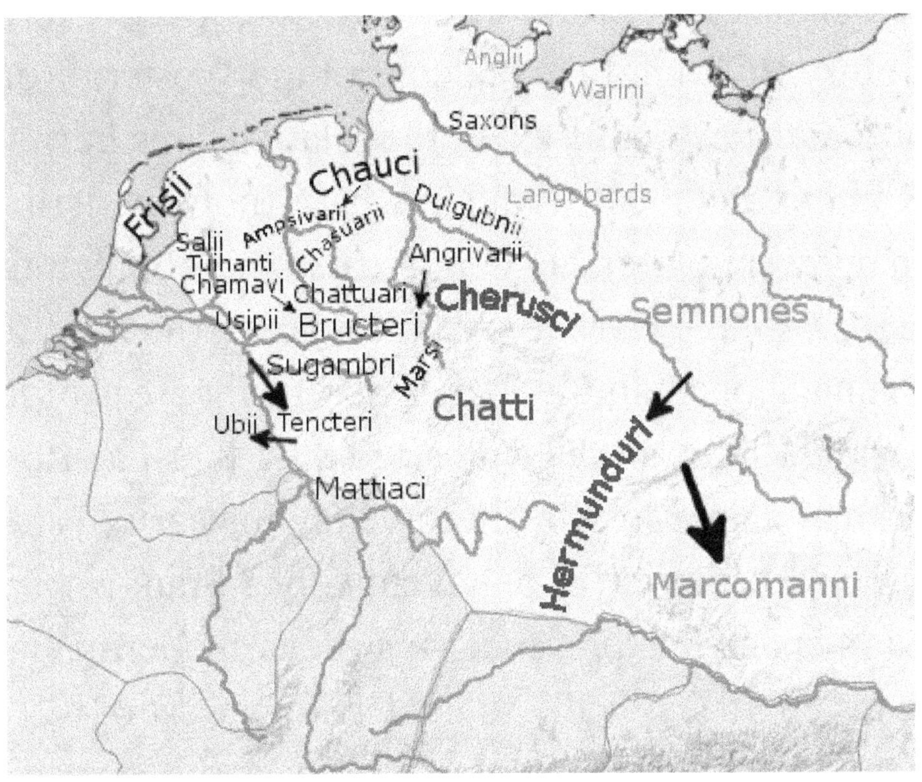

Andrw Lancaster's map of the region in antiquity

"[The] largest and the most warlike nation of all the Germans." – Caesar's description of the Suebi

Despite all the accomplishments and widespread victories and conquests that the ancient Romans accrued over the centuries, one of their most critical failures was the inability to subjugate Germany. Indeed, historians have singled out this one failure as central to the ultimate downfall of Rome, as the constant wars against the Germanic tribes and the need to defend the frontier on the Rhine helped bring the Roman Empire to its knees.

There are elements of truth in such a conclusion, but the reality was far more fluid than is often realized. From the 1st century BCE until the collapse of the Western Roman Empire in the 5th century CE, the relationships between the Romans and those living in what is now modern Germany were extremely complicated, involving much more than simple warfare. As a Roman territory, Germania at one point included significant areas of land east of the Rhine, all the way up to the Elbe. The Romans would maintain a significant force on this eastern side until the 3rd century CE, but eventually a Frankish invasion ended that presence, and the term Germania came to refer specifically to the territory west of the Rhine, which included the two provinces of Germania Superior and Germania Inferior, or Upper and Lower Germany. Those provinces were key to the defense of the empire, so much so that Triers provided the location of one of the four seats of government near the end of Rome's reign.

The people that came to be known as Germans originally came from Scandinavia and were mainly shepherds and hunters, but they comprised a number of distinct groups. Within each group, there were separate tribes, and as their populations grew, the land they occupied in Scandinavia was unable to support them, so they began migrating south, settling outside the borders of the Roman Empire.

The Germans were fierce warriors who employed rather crude but effective tactics in battle. Their main approach was one of charging directly at an enemy and fighting hand-to-hand using their long swords and shields. Body armor was unknown, and they wore only animal-skins. Most warriors wore their hair long, dyed red and greased into ponytails.

Friction between Rome and the German tribes can be traced back as far as 113 BCE, and the next 500 years brought full-scale campaigns by the Romans against the various individual tribes, resulting in numerous battles and constant uprisings wherever any part of the land east of the Rhine was occupied for any length of time. The impact of this constant warfare on both sides cannot be underestimated, and all the while, the fighting and other interactions had massive cultural and political influences going in both directions.

The Germans who lived on Gaul's side of the Rhine proved to be more amenable to Roman culture and were willing to ally with and even give obedience to the Romans, but those who lived north of the Rhine were completely recalcitrant and obstinate when it came to any outsiders, Roman or otherwise. Rebellions among the Celts in Gaul (roughly equivalent to modern France) in 59 BCE forced Caesar to lead a major campaign into the province, which ultimately resulted in the suppression of the Celts, but the Germans north of the Rhine remained independent. Although Caesar led two secondary campaigns across the Rhine against the Germans, both were unsuccessful.

Among the Germans who stymied Caesar's plans, those who gave the Romans the most problems were the Suebi. Caesar's account of his Gallic campaign included the first documented account of the Suebi, who were described as fearless warriors, yet wholly uncivilized and barbaric in the eyes of the Romans. The Suebi lived north of the Rhine for hundreds of years, mostly unaffected by Rome's expansion, and while the Romans and the Suebi did have early contact with each other, those contacts were relatively inconsequential. It was not until the Suebi took part in the great migrations that ravaged Europe in the 5th century CE that they had a more immediate impact on Rome.

By then, the Suebi had branched into many sub-tribes. The group that attacked Gaul and settled in the Iberian Peninsula became known as the Sueves. The Sueves eventually integrated with other people in Iberia, while the Suebi who stayed behind in Germany became known as the Swabians in the Middle Ages.

The Suebi: The History and Legacy of the Ancient

Ancient Germania

Although there were scores of different tribes that participated in migrations across Europe in antiquity, modern scholars have divided the Germanic peoples into the West Germans and East Germans. The West Germans originated somewhere in Eastern Europe and pressed westward from between the Oder and Elbe Rivers until they displaced the more culturally sophisticated, but less warlike Celts, east of the Rhine, and north of the Main rivers, around 200 BCE. The West Germans, perhaps influenced by the Celts who they replaced, adopted a more sedentary lifestyle and culture, and farming and cooperation with the Romans became common. It was to these Germans that Julius Caesar and the Roman historian Tacitus described in detail in their written works.

The amount of pressure the West Germans placed on the Roman Empire was negligible, but their cousins, the East Germans, entered the scene later with much more bluster and violence. The East Germans migrated into continental Europe from Scandinavia sometime between 600 and 300 BCE, and almost immediately they proved to be much more of a problem for the Romans than their West German cousins. The Vandals, Goths, and Gepids were the most notable of the East German tribes, who early in their migrations followed a southerly route that took them to the shores of the Black Sea and the banks of the

Danube River by the 3rd century CE. The migrations appear to have followed an organized pattern, at least from the perspective of the Germanic tribes, which is further confirmed by the sophisticated styles of government they used during the period.

Today, many have the idea that the leaders of the German tribes truly lived up to their epithet "barbarians," as each king was thought to rule over his people with the iron hand of an autocrat. The reality is that some of the Germanic peoples practiced sophisticated forms of government, as numerous and diverse as the people themselves. Some of these tribes operated as republics, not much different than Rome's, while others were monarchies, but even the Germanic republics recognized the importance of a chieftain and warlord, and elected kings. This assembly of freemen that was, for all intents and purposes, a republic in the truest sense, was preserved for centuries and better documented by the Norse in Scandinavia. Essentially, the assembly of freemen within any of the tribes was considered sovereign, and the king, or graf, could do nothing without their counsel. The difference between the king and graf was minor, and only due to the origins of the leader, not how he functioned. The graf was a chieftain elected from among the freemen, while the king was elected from the members of a particular family considered to possess noble blood. The functions of both the graf and the king were the same, however: to lead his people into battle. It was on the battlefield that the Germanic tribes distinguished themselves both as allies and enemies of the Roman Empire.

The Romans referred to the lands beyond the Rhine and Danube as Germania, which roughly corresponds to the borders of modern Germany and parts of Switzerland and the Netherlands. They referred to the people of the region generally as Germans, but usually they assigned each tribe a Latinized version of their German names.

Some of those ancient names are still apparent today in place names, and Swabia is a geographic region in southern Germany that received its name from sub-tribes of the ancient Suebi who lived there. Alemanni was another name for the Suebi and is today the basis for the name of the German people in most modern Romance languages. For the Romans, these Germans were generally a mysterious people whose seeming savagery both awed and repulsed them.

The name "Suebi" is a Latin approximation of the name the tribe called themselves, but as was the case with nearly everything the Romans did in relation to non-Roman people, they "Romanized" or "Latinized" the name. The Suebi were a Germanic people who were part of the general migration of Germanic people out of Scandinavia, and once they entered what is today Germany, they began forming tribes and ethnic groups. The land the Suebi inhabited was just to the north of the Rhine River's delta and east of the lower Rhine in what is today the Netherlands.

Tacitus, one of the foremost Roman historians of the 1st century CE, wrote a general description of what the Romans considered the boundaries of Germania: "The whole of Germany is thus bounded; separated from Gaul, from Rhoetia and Pannonia, by the rivers Rhine and Danube; from Sarmatia and Dacia by mutual fear, or by high mountains: the rest is encompassed by the ocean, which forms huge bays, and comprehends a tract of islands immense in extent: for we have lately known certain nations and kingdoms there, such as the war discovered. The Rhine rising in the Rhoetian Alps from a summit altogether rocky and perpendicular, after a small winding towards the west, is lost in the Northern Ocean. The Danube issues out of the mountain Abnoba, one very high but very easy of ascent, and traversing several nations, falls by six streams into the Euxine Sea; for its seventh channel is absorbed in the Fenns." (Tacitus, *Germania*, I).

The Suebi shared this region with dozens of other major tribes and perhaps hundreds of smaller sub-tribes. By then, Julius Caesar had offered a more detailed account of the Suebi and their territory over 150 years earlier. When Caesar campaigned in Gaul to subdue recalcitrant Celtic tribes from 58-52 BCE, he also crossed the Rhine for two brief campaigns against the Suebi. Since Caesar was a writer as well as a general and politician, he recorded the events in his *Commentarii de Bello Gallico,* which also offered a general geographic description of Gaul and the small region of Germania he visited. He wrote that the Suebi inhabited a vast region and could call a fairly large army into the field: "The Suebi are by far the largest and most warlike of the German nations. It is said that they have a hundred cantons, each of which provides annually a thousand armed men for service in foreign wars." (Caesar, *Commentarii de Bello Gallico*, IV, I).

A Roman statuette of a Suebi captive

An ancient bust of Caesar

This passage raises some important questions about Caesar's scholarship and the sources he used to compile his historical and geographical study.

As will be discussed later, Caesar did not spend very much time in Suebi territory, certainly not enough to traverse "a hundred cantons" of territory, which raises the question of how he came to this number. Since he did have contacts with other Germanic tribes that were variously at war or allied with the Suebi, as well as Celtic tribes who regularly dealt with them, it is likely that he was given this information by one or more of those sources. It certainly raises questions concerning the veracity of the claim, or Caesar's sources for the claim, but it does appear the Suebi did inhabit a large area nonetheless. Caesar noted that the Suebi controlling such a large area was contingent upon their martial culture and philosophy and was, in some ways, part of their religion.

According to Caesar, the land of the Suebi was relatively undeveloped, which the Suebi took as a badge of honor. They protected their borders and themselves by leaving as much land as possible uninhabited and unused. Caesar explained, "They regard it as the proudest glory of a nation to keep the largest possible area round its frontiers uninhabited, because it shows that many other people are inferior to it in military might. It is said, for example, that on one side of the Suebic territory, the country is uninhabited for a distance of more than five hundred and fifty miles. On the other side, their nearest neighbors are the Ubii, who were once – by German standards – a considerable and prosperous nation… The Suebi, after repeated attempts to oust them from their home by force of arms, found them too numerous and strong to be dispossessed, but compelled them to pay tribute and greatly reduce their pride and power." (Caesar, *Commentarii de Bello Gallico*, IV, 3).

The fact that the Suebi were a strong and warlike tribe that existed during the rise of the Roman Empire cannot be denied, but defining who exactly the Suebi were is a bit more complicated. As will be discussed further below, the Suebi were known by different names at different points in history, which suggests that they were possibly more of a coalition or confederacy than one single tribe. Indeed, the various ancient German tribes frequently coalesced into confederations that would sometimes become one people, or at least viewed as one people. Perhaps the best known of these confederacies was the one the Angles, Saxons, and Jutes formed when they sailed from mainland Europe to Britain in the 5th century CE. Ancient sources, including Tacitus, seem to indicate that the Jutes formed a confederacy with other tribes before they left continental Europe for Britain, indicating that such arrangements were perhaps not uncommon (Tacitus, *Germania*, II, 40).

Other Germanic alliances/confederacies formed before, some of which involved the Suebi. According to Tacitus, the Suebi, whom he referred to as the "Suevians," were comprised of several different tribes or "nations." He noted, "I must now proceed to speak of the Suevians, who are not, like the Cattans and Tencterians, comprehended in a single people; but divided into several nations all bearing distinct names, though in general they are entitled Suevians, and occupy the larger share of Germany. This people are remarkable for a peculiar custom, that of twisting their hair and binding it up in a knot. It is thus the Suevians are distinguished from the other Germans, thus the free Suevians from their slaves. In other nations, whether from alliance of blood with the Suevians, or, as is usual, from imitation, this practice is also found, yet rarely, and never exceeds the years of youth. The Suevians, even when their hair is white through age, continue to raise it backwards in a manner stern and staring; and often tie it upon the top of their head only. That of their Princes, is more accurately disposed, and so far they study to appear agreeable and comely; but without any culpable intention. For by it, they mean not to make love or to incite it: they thus dress when proceeding to war, and deck their heads so as to add to their height and terror in the eyes of the enemy." (Tacitus, *Germania*, II).

The passage appears to indicate that apart from the distinct way the Suebi wore their hair, there was considerable diversity among the people, possibly due to the fact that they controlled most of Germany. It should also be pointed out that Tacitus considered a wider section of Germania than Caesar did, and that the Suebi who lived closest to the Rhine were culturally different in many ways than those who lived further in the interior.

The Germans that Caesar met were still very much influenced by the region's original Celtic inhabitants. Both sides of the Rhine River at the time were still very Celtic culturally speaking, with most of the place names being derived from Celtic words and even most of the tribes, including the Germans, having names that were Latin approximations of Celtic designations. Only the Suebi had a Latin name that was derived directly from German, proof that their arrival in the region came much later (Schadee 2008, 162). With that said, it is likely that as much as the Suebi attempted to prevent foreign influences from entering their tribes, those closest to the Rhine (the ones Caesar had contact with) were influenced by the Celts in many ways and were different than the Suebi who lived deeper in Germania. This would explain the diversity of the Suebi who Tacitus described, and it would also explain how and why some of the Suebi later left Germany while others stayed. Again, this would be in keeping with the idea of a confederacy that was led by the Suebi, with other tribes taking the same name or being designated as Suebi despite not necessarily sharing the same origins.

The first major confrontation between Roman forces and local tribes became known as the Cimbrian War and lasted from 113-101 BCE. The Cimbri were the most numerous of several related tribes (including the Teutons, the Ambrones, and the Tigurini) that had been migrating south from their overcrowded homelands in Jutland and the areas around the North Sea since approximately 120 BCE. Strabo dismissed the common theory that the migration had been sparked by extensive flooding, but regardless of the reasons, by 113 BCE they had reached the Danube. They attacked the local Taurisci, who immediately called on their Roman allies to assist in their defense.[1]

When the Cimbri tribes attempted to cross into Roman territory, and thus seemingly threatened Italy, this propelled the Senate into action. The campaign for the Romans was led by Gnaeus Papirius Carbo,[2] who took up a defensive position in Noricum, the capital of the Taurisci. He demanded that the tribes withdraw, and the Germans, presumably concerned about Roman military power, seem to have initially complied. However, when they discovered that the Romans planned to ambush them on their retreat, they turned around and went on the offensive instead.

At the Battle of Noreia, they annihilated Carbo's army, although he was able to escape.[3] This decisive victory

---

[1] Strabo, *Geographica*, VII, 2.

[2] Elected Consul in 113 B.C.

[3] Carbo eventually committed suicide, choosing this over exile after being found guilty of provoking and then losing the Battle of Noreia (see Cicero, *Epistulae ad Familiares (Letter to Friends),*. IX.2; Livy, *Periochae,* 63.

cleared the way for the tribes to directly invade Italy, but for reasons still unexplained, they decided instead to turn west into Gaul. There, they invaded Gallia Narbonensis in 109 BCE and defeated the Roman army under Marcus Junius Silanus.[4] The Romans suffered further major defeats in 107 BCE at the Battle of Agen and the Battle of Burdigalla, when the consul, Lucius Cassius Longinus Ravalla, was killed.[5] In 105 BCE, Rome sent consul Gnaeus Mallius Maximus[6] and the proconsul, Quintus Servilius Caepio,[7] with the largest force assembled since the Punic Wars to confront the tribesmen. Estimates put the army at 80,000 fighting men, with thousands of additional support personnel, all organized into two armies.

The two men did not get on well, so much so that they marched separately to the base camps on the River Rhone at Vaucluse. They also made the fatal mistake of setting up camps on opposite sides of the river. Not only did this division of forces leave them weakened, but Caepio, determined to have all the glory, attacked the tribesmen without the support of Maximus. His force was totally destroyed and his camp overrun.[8] The Germans then turned their attention to Maximus, whose force was just as

---

[4] Elected Consul in 109 B.C. (for the defeat, see Livy, *Periochae,* 65.

[5] Elected Consul in 107 B.C.

[6] Elected in 105 B.C.

[7] Elected in 106 B.C.

[8] p. 125, *The Storm before the Storm: The Beginning of the End of the Roman Republic by M. Duncan (2017). New York: Public Affairs.*

easily dispatched.[9]

Both commanders managed to escape the battlefield with a few of their own guards, but the Battle of Arausio was the greatest defeat inflicted on the Roman legions since Hannibal annihilated the Roman forces at the Battle of Cannae during the Second Punic War. Once again, the defeat left Italy once again wide open to invasion, but the Cimbri did not take their opportunity to invade. Instead, they moved even further west into Hispania, where, at the hands of the Celtiberians, they suffered their first major defeat.[10] Their allies, the Teutones, had decided to stay in Gaul. However, they too declined to take advantage of the opportunity created by the victory at Arausio.

From a Roman perspective, this war had particular significance because the conflict helped propel Roman general and statesman Gaius Marius (157 BCE–86 BCE) to prominence. His successes provided the basis for the political power that he used to reform the Roman army and many of the political practices of the Republic.[11] The most significant of these many reforms was in direct response to the threat from the German tribes. His complete reorganization of the Roman legions proved critical in enabling Rome to defend itself in the north and

---

[9] Pp. 66–72, 'The Revolution' in *The History of Rome, Book IV (Vols I–V)* by T. Mommsen (1854). The Free Press.

[10] Livy, Periochae, LXVII

[11] p. 135, *The Storm before the Storm: The Beginning of the End of the Roman Republic* by M. Duncan (2017). New York: PublicAffairs).

expand its territory in Africa and the Middle East. That reason alone would make Marius's rise to power important, but he also played a significant role in the relationship between Rome and the Germanic tribes.[12]

A bust of Marius

While Marius reformed the Roman forces, the Cimbri – following their defeat in Spain – had rallied and pushed further into northern Gaul to join their allies the Teutons.

---

[12] Plutarch, *Life of Marius.*

It was now, finally, that the united tribes decided the time had come to invade Italy. They marched through Switzerland and Savoy, picking up further allies among the Helvetians, thus enabling them to split their force into two. The plan was for the Teutons and Helvetians to invade Cisalpine Gaul, while the Cimbri would enter through the Julian and Carnic Alps.

Marius had set up camp at Valence. The Teutons, along with the Ambrones, attacked him there, but without success. As they were unable to lure Marius into pitched battle, they decided to simply march around his encampment, and so enormous were their numbers that they reportedly took nearly a week to do so.[13] However, as the tribesmen marched south, the Romans shadowed them and, at a place more favorable to them, near Aquae Sextiae, Marius engineered an ambush. The Teutonic forces were totally destroyed, and their king was captured.

Marius now had to deal with the Cimbri, who had passed virtually unopposed into northern Italy and had systematically begun plundering the countryside. Marius's co-consul, Quintus Lutatius Catulus,[14] had failed to fortify the Alpine passes and retreated beyond the River Po into northern Italy. The invaders were under the command of the Cimbri king, Boirix, who had secured victory against

---

[13] p. 54, *The Gracchi, Marius, and Sulla Epochs of Ancient History by* A. H. Beesely (2011). Amazon Digital Services.

[14] Elected as Consul in 102 B.C.

the Romans at the Battle of Arausio at Vercellae in July 101 BCE.

Ultimately the new legions demonstrated their superiority and the tribesmen were almost totally annihilated. The women and children subsequently committed suicide to avoid falling into Roman hands.[15]

The political consequences of this war were both immediate and lasting for Rome. In the longer term, remnants of the Cimbri who had not migrated south continued to live in northern Jutland and southern Scandinavia, and some of their near relatives settled in southern Gaul and Germania. Their descendants would have to confront Julius Caesar, Marius's nephew, in his legendary Gallic campaigns.

---

[15] Plutarch, *Life of Marius*, XXVII.2.

The Gallic Wars

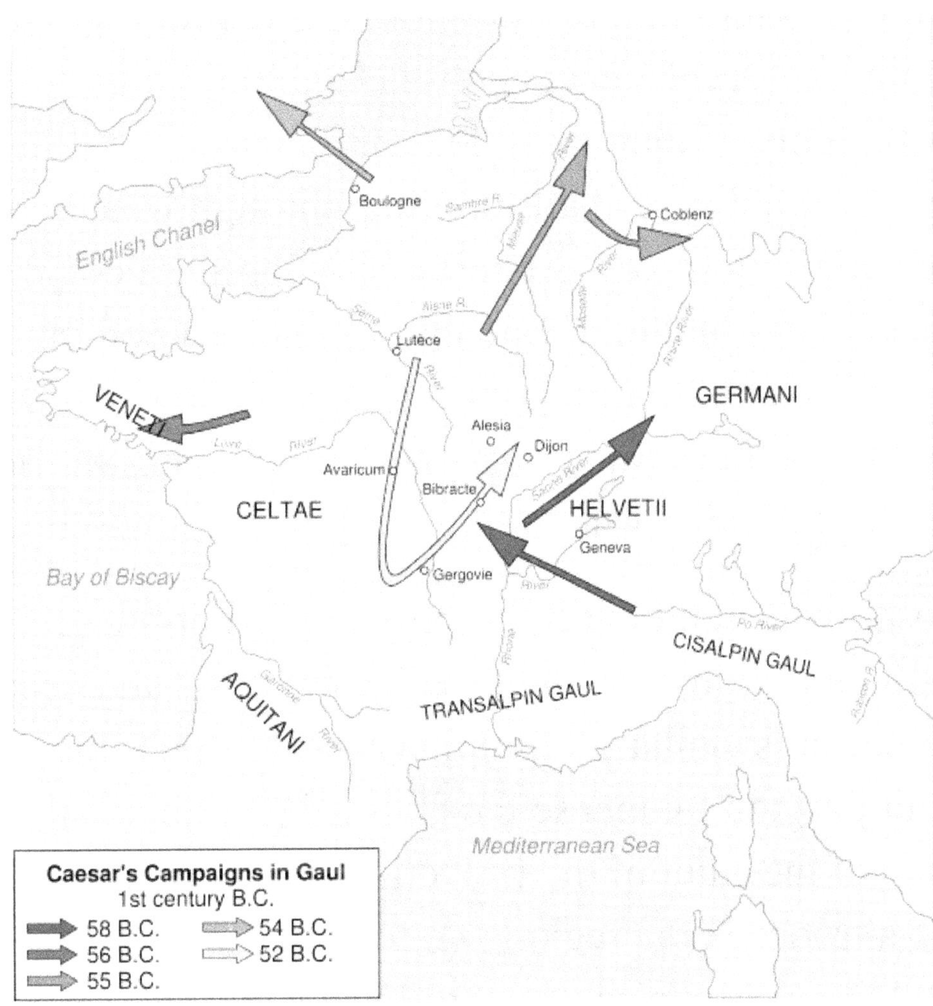

A map of Caesar's campaigns

In the early months of 58 BCE, the Helvetii, a Gaulish tribe inhabiting the lands abutting Gallia Transalpina, were pressured into seeking new lands by the fractious Germans now assailing their borders and conducting raids on their territory. As a result, they began a mass migration, destroying their homesteads as they began to march southwards. Although their destination lay outside of Roman territory and thus might not have affected the

Romans to any great extent, their chosen route took them via modern Geneva into the lands of the Allobroges, a tribe under direct Roman control. This was a concern, because it meant there were tens of thousands of potentially bellicose Gauls crossing through what was in effect Roman territory. At best, the Allobroges could expect to have anything valuable which lay upon the Helvetii's line of march to go missing, while worst-case scenarios included raids by high-spirited young warriors or even a full-scale war.

Caesar, who at the time was pursuing his political ambitions in Rome, was notified of the crisis and headed north towards Gallia Transalpina as fast as possible. With only one legion to oppose the Helvetii (the personal retinue of the chief of the Helvetii alone outnumbered the Roman troops in the region two to one), Caesar was forced to quickly raise a levy of local auxiliaries. He then marched his troops to the strategic lynchpin of the region: the bridge over the Rhone. Caesar knew that the Helvetii must cross the Rhone at some point to continue their march westwards, and the easiest place for them to do so, slowed down by women and children as they were, was the bridge that had been built where the Rhone emptied into Lake Geneva. To thwart them, Caesar ordered it destroyed.

The advancing horde of the Helvetii arrived in sight of

Geneva to find the bridge destroyed and a sizeable part of Caesar's forces encamped upon the far bank. High-ranking emissaries were immediately dispatched to Caesar by the Helvetii, ostensibly in an attempt to try and negotiate a peaceful passage. However, rather than entertain these dignitaries, Caesar stalled them for two weeks, using that time to recruit a large contingent of mercenary cavalry from the neighboring tribe of the Remi. He also bolstered his levies with slingers and javelineers, and more importantly, he had his legionaries complete a massive series of siege works. Without the bridge across the Rhone, the only place the Helvetii could proceed along their journey was through the Pas de l'Ecluse, a dangerous route which they had initially decided to avoid but was now their only hope. Caesar's fortifications aimed to deny this to them as well; his men constructed a rampart nearly 20 feet high and almost 20 miles long, reinforced by fortifications and fronted by a deep ditch, heavily garrisoned all along its length.

For the Helvetii, there was no way forward without a fight.

Caesar, secure in his position, was able to refuse the Helvetii's overtures, and once the Helvetii became desperate enough, they attempted to launch a series of attacks across the river, only to have Caesar's troops repulse them with ease. The Helvetii would have to turn away, but whatever path they chose would still take them through lands belonging to Roman allies, and they were unlikely to be inclined to be peaceful. Caesar, sensing an opportunity for a campaign that would win him laurels and plunder and extend Rome's influence further to the north and west, resolved to come to their aid. Leaving his legion near Geneva, he hurried to Aquileia (in modern northwest Italy near the border with France) and took command of the three legions stationed there, raising Legio XI and Legio XII Fulminata as reinforcements. With about 25,000 men under his command, Caesar then marched north and elected to take the most direct route, confident that even though he had to cross hostile territory, his strength was enough to see any enemy attack off.

Despite being harassed by local tribes, Caesar was able to catch the Helvetii on the march as they attempted to ford the Avar River. The bulk of the Helvetii had already made it onto the far bank via improvised rafts and ferries, but a large portion of them remained on the near bank of the Avar. With three legions under his command, Caesar fell upon this rearguard and destroyed it.

In the wake of this victory, Caesar constructed a bridge across the Agar and set off in pursuit of the Helvetii. The Helvetii once again attempted to negotiate, but Caesar refused their overtures. His pursuit had now brought him deep into Aedui territory, so he was forced to negotiate with their chieftain Dumnorix for supplies for his men. Dumnorix, however, proved ambivalent at best in his support, and although a number of his cavalrymen served with Caesar's army, his promised supplies were not forthcoming. Rather than march his army into the ground, Caesar gave up his pursuit and headed for Bribacte, an Aedui stronghold, to demand the promised supplies at swordpoint.

However, the Helvetii had been emboldened by this apparent retreat and by an earlier reversal suffered by Caesar's Roman and Aedui cavalry at the hands of a smaller Helvetii mounted unit. With supplies running dangerously low and the Helvetii snapping at his rearguard's heels, Caesar chose to make his stand near the town of Bibracte in mid-June 58 BC. By this point, Caesar had six full legions under his command, plus auxiliaries. In the climactic battle between the two sides, Caesar's men drove the Helvetii back nearly to their own baggage train, until they were in turn attacked in the flanks by a relief force of the Boii and Tulingi tribes arriving late to the battle. At this point, Caesar ordered his foremost elements to press on their attack, committing his reserve to fending off the Boii and Tulingi. The battle lasted for the better part of a day, but by evening Caesar was master of the field, and he had captured quite a few important prisoners.

According to Caesar's estimates, his 30,000 men had faced the better part of 90,000 enemy combatants, many of whom lay dead or dying on the battlefield. The remnants of the Helvetii, including tens of thousands of women and children, took refuge with a neighboring tribe, as Caesar and his men were not initially in a position to pursue them. However, once he had tended to his wounded, Caesar pushed on and was able to persuade the Helvetii to surrender.

In the wake of his victory against the Helvetii, Caesar quickly became aware that he had forged a reputation throughout all of Gaul as a great general. He was approached by a congress of tribes, both allied and notionally neutral, who entreated him to deal with the problem of a leader named Ariovistus and his trespassing Suebi. The Suebi's encroachment was possibly part of the reason the Helvetii had decided to decamp from their ancestral lands in the first place.

Caesar had plenty of incentive to undertake such a campaign; not only would it strengthen his standing with the Aedui and potentially bring other Gaulish tribes into the fold, it would also allow him the opportunity to expand Rome's borders into the lands held by the Suebi, cement his status among his legionaries as a successful general, increase his haul of plunder, and overtake Pompey the Great in the eyes of the Roman people and the Senate as Rome's foremost commander. On top of all that, the Gauls who approached Caesar also warned during negotiations that should Caesar refuse to aid them, they might well be forced to migrate, possibly even into Roman-controlled territory. Accordingly, Caesar marched.

Ignoring the fact that Ariovistus had been declared a "friend of the Roman people" by the Senate in 59 BC, Caesar took advantage of the Suebi's breaching of an ultimatum he had posed (no more incursions across the Rhine) as his *casus belli*. Having received intelligence that Ariovistus planned to seize Vesontio, the Sequani's capital, Caesar ordered his legions to force-march towards the city, knowing it was imperative that he reach it before Ariovistus and his army. When several of his newly raised legions proved slow on the march, as the men were not hardened to such marching, Caesar proved himself a master at understanding the psychology of military morale by making a public speech to his men, claiming that only his personally raised Legio X was up to scratch. Desperate to prove him wrong, the men of the other legions outdid themselves on the march, with the result that Caesar reached the town of Vesontio before Ariovistus could.

Of course, Caesar wasn't terribly worried by such boasts. With the armies of the Suebi facing Caesar's legions across the plain of Vesontio, Ariovistus asked Caesar for a meeting, but this fell through when some soldiers from Ariovistus's army began hurling stones at Caesar's escort. Ariovistus attempted to negotiate a new meeting, but Caesar chose to send two fairly junior officers instead. Enraged by this perceived slight, Ariovistus had the pair imprisoned, then marched his army around Caesar's and parked it so that it straddled Caesar's lines of communication and supply with his Gaulish allies. When Caesar attempted to offer battle, Ariovistus refused to commit his armies to the fray, so to entice him into fighting, Caesar deliberately divided his force, placing a smaller part of it inside a fortified camp close to the Suebi's lines. The Suebi attacked this unit but were repulsed, and Caesar described the aftermath of that small skirmish: "Then at last Ariovistus sent part of his forces to attack the lesser camp. The battle was vigorously maintained on both sides till the evening. At sunset, after many wounds had been inflicted and received, Ariovistus led back his forces into camp. When Caesar inquired of his prisoners, wherefore Ariovistus did not come to an engagement, he discovered this to be the reason-that among the Germans it was the custom for their matrons to pronounce from lots and divination, whether it were expedient that the battle should be engaged in or not; that they had said, 'that it was not the will of heaven that the Germans should conquer, if they engaged in battle before the new moon.'"

The following morning, Caesar advanced the bulk of his army in the customary triple rank against Ariovistus, who deployed his warriors in seven echelons. Caesar himself took command of the right flank. The battle was joined, and quickly turned into a slugging match, with neither side being able to win a clear advantage. Caesar again described the fighting in graphic detail: "There were found very many of our soldiers who leaped upon the phalanx, and with their hands tore away the shields, and wounded the enemy from above. Although the army of the enemy was routed on the left wing and put to flight, they pressed heavily on our men from the right wing, by the great number of their troops."

After several hours of confused fighting, the Suebi had succeeded in bending back the Roman left flank almost to the breaking point. At this point, one of Caesar's officers, Publius Crassus (son of the triumvirate Marcus Crassus), led a perfectly timed cavalry charge to smash into the flank of the Suebi advance on the Roman left, then ordered forward the reserve to reverse the attack of Ariovistus's men into a rout. The Romans then rolled up the Germanic line from their left, at which point the Suebi broke and fled. Tens of thousands were cut down in the ensuing slaughter as the broken lines of Ariovistus's men attempted to flee the battlefield (Caesar estimates

120,000, but this is likely high). Ariovistus and the shattered remnants of his army retreated across the Rhine and would never threaten Gaul again. As Caesar proudly put it in *De Bello Gallico*, "Caesar having concluded two very important wars in one campaign, conducted his army into winter quarters among the Sequani, a little earlier than the season of the year required."

In the winter of 56-55 BCE, Caesar met the Usipetes and Tenctheri Germanic tribes when they crossed the Rhine to parlay with the Romans (Brown 2014, 392). Caesar willingly met with the tribal leaders because he saw it as a potential opportunity to bring more tribes under the Roman rule, and he figured they could also potentially provide the Romans with much needed intelligence of northern Gaul and Germania. According to Caesar, they had moved to the region due to the bellicose and expansionist Suebi.

The Upietes and Tenctheri were in the same predicament. For many years they withstood the Suebi's pressure, but eventually they were driven from their country. After wandering for three years in many parts of Germany, they reached the Rhine in the territory of the Menapii, who had lands, farmhouses, and villages on both banks of the river. The parlay went well at first, with the Germans initially agreeing to a truce and to slow their advance into the territory. The Romans were not really in a position of strength, as the region was for, the most part, unknown to them and they did not know the strength of their potential adversaries, so the Romans accepted the Germans' agreement. The Germans, though, took the opportunity to take the initiative with a sneak attack, using tactics that the Suebi would also use later against the Romans. Caesar wrote, "Our men, who thought themselves safe from attack because the enemy's envoys had only just left Caesar and had asked for a truce for that day, were at first thrown into disorder. When they rallied, the German horsemen, following their usual practice, jumped down, unhorsed a number of our men by stabbing their horses in the belly, put the rest to flight, and kept them on the run in such a panic that they did not stop until they came in sight of the marching column of infantry." (Caesar, *Commentarii de Bello Gallico*, IV, 12).

The Roman response was quick, efficient, and vicious. Caesar ordered his men to attack the Germans in the camps and not to spare women or children. According to Caesar, "The Roman soldiers could tell that they were afraid by their cries and hurried movements, and, spurred on by the recollection of the previous day's treachery, burst into the camp. Those of the Germans, who were quick enough in seizing their weapons, resisted for a time, fighting under cover of their wagons and baggage. But there was also a great crowd of women and children in the camp, for they had brought all their families with them when they left home and crossed the Rhine. These people began to flee in all directions, and were hunted down by the cavalry which Caesar sent out for that purpose." (Caesar, *Commentarii de Bello Gallico*, IV, 14).

Caesar and the Romans had defeated the Upietes and Tenctheri, but they also intended to annihilate them completely. Many of those German refugees fled right into the territory of the Suebi, who they knew and respected. Even years after the Suebi drove the Upietes and Tenctheri from their homeland, according to Caesar the latter still feared and respected the former, apparently more so than they did the Romans. The Romans were far off from the Upietes and Tenctheri, even the Romans in Gaul, while the Suebi represented a more immediate threat. The Upietes and Tenctheri even told Caesar the following: "The only people whose superiority we acknowledge are the Suebi, with whom the gods themselves cannot compete. There is no one else on earth that we cannot conquer." (Caesar, *Commentarii de Bello Gallico*, IV, 9).

As a result, when the German refugees crossed the Rhine, Caesar presumed that it was to seek the protection of the Suebi. By that time, Caesar had already dealt with the Suebi on Gaul's side of the Rhine, so he was somewhat familiar with them and their tactics, although he was not yet familiar with their land in Germania. The Romans would later learn that although the land of the Suebi was not particularly developed, at least by Roman standards, it was well-protected.

Although Caesar may have eliminated the immediate German threat in Gaul by defeating Ariovistus, the Suebi and their allies were still a threat across the Rhine, and Caesar was always looking for ways to enhance his reputation and expand Rome's borders, so he immediately began looking to Germania. It is reasonable to conclude that Caesar viewed the Suebi as a major threat to Rome's plans in Gaul in 56 BCE, because even as Vercingetorix's Celtic coalition was giving the Romans more problems than they could handle at the time, Caesar still made plans to cross the Rhine and destroy the Suebi and their allies.

In late 56 or early 55 BCE, Caesar made the momentous decision to be the first Roman to bridge the Rhine River and enter Germania. This "discovery" was actually quite incredible for the time, and it could be compared with Magellan's circumnavigation of the globe more than 1,500 years later given the way it expanded the map and geographic knowledge the Romans had of the world. Caesar wrote that there were three reasons for the expedition, the first of which was a preemptive strike against the Suebi and other Germanic tribes to make them "less inclined to come over into Gaul" (Caesar,

Commentarii de Bello Gallico, IV, 16). The second reason was to hunt down refugees, or "fugitives" as he called them, from the previous battle against the Suebi and their allies on the Gaul side of the Rhine. The final reason directly involved the Suebi: "A third reason was that the Ubii – the only people in Germany who had sent envoys to Caesar, entered into alliance with him, and given hostages – were earnestly entreating him to come and defend them from the oppression of the Suebi or, if the public business with which he was occupied made that impossible, merely to bring his army across the river, which would suffice to deliver them from immediate danger and assure their security for the future." (Caesar, *Commentarii de Bello Gallico*, IV, 16).

Caesar did not offer details of the nature of the relationship the Romans had with the Ubii, such as how and when it came to be, other than that they resided on the Germania side of the Rhine and were enemies of the Suebi. The Roman general also did not relate many logistical details about the campaign, although it can be reasonably assumed that the Romans did not penetrate far into Germania. The Ubii apparently acted as scouts and spies for the Romans, sending them towards the Suebi's villages and camps.

After learning where the Suebi were located, Caesar had his legions attack their villages, but the Romans found them empty. After the Romans burned the villages as a show of force, Caesar learned that the Suebi had devised their own strategy to deal with the Roman invaders. Referring to himself in the third person, he wrote, "Caesar remained for a few days in their territory, burning all the villages and farm buildings and cutting down the crops, and then returned to the Ubii, to whom he promised help to if they were molested by the Suebi. They informed him that the Suebi, on learning from their scouts that a bridge was under construction, had convened a council – their usual procedure in such cases – and sent out word in all directions that the people should abandon their towns and hide their wives and children and property in the forests. All men capable of bearing arms had been ordered to assemble in one place, almost exactly in the middle of their territory. There they were awaiting the Romans, and had determined to fight a decisive battle on the spot. On receiving this news, Caesar re-crossed the bridge into Gaul and destroyed it behind him." (Caesar, *Commentarii de Bello Gallico*, IV, 19).

Caesar likely knew that his forces were outnumbered by the Suebi, and given that the Romans forces were in unfamiliar and hostile territory, it made little sense to take any risks. Thus, while declaring he had accomplished his mission, Caesar returned to Gaul.

After crossing back into Gaul, Caesar spent more than a

year campaigning against Vercingetorix and his coalition and even sent an expedition to Britain, but the Suebi and Germania were never far from his mind. The fluid geopolitical situation in Gaul changed again in 53 BCE when the Treveri, who were up until that time pro-Roman and anti-Suebi, rebelled against the Romans. According to Caesar, tribes on the Germania side of the Rhine sent aid to the Treveri, prompting him to lead a second campaign across the Rhine: "After marching from the country of the Menapii to that of the Treveri, Caesar determined to cross the Rhine for two reasons: first, because the Germans had sent the Treveri reinforcements to use against him; secondly, to prevent Ambiorix finding an asylum in Germany. He therefore proceeded to build a bridge a little above the place where he had crossed before." (Caesar, *Commentarii de Bello Gallico*, VI, 9).

Caesar's pursuit of the rebel Ambiorix was certainly the *casus belli* for the campaign, but modern historians believe he may have added those two reasons to his writings later, while the primary objective was to conquer Germania (Schadee 2008, 170). The conquest of Germania definitely would have been an incredibly ambitious campaign, but the rewards were high and the potential costs were low. Theoretically, if the campaign failed, Caesar could simply take his forces back over the Rhine and focus on his initial objectives in Gaul.

Caesar may have been emboldened from his first foray into Germania years earlier, perhaps believing that the tactics he used then could be employed even more successfully a second time. His legions were also more experienced and hardened from continual fighting in Gaul, and he may have believed that his Ubii allies were more reliable than they were. The problem was that the Ubii had to live in Germania with the Suebi, while the Romans could leave at any time. Apparently, the situation became quite untenable for the Ubii, who appealed to Caesar to send troops. He responded by telling them to gather their supplies, prepare for a siege, and wait for the arrival of the Romans. According to Caesar, however, the Suebi decided to wait as well: "The Ubii carried out these instructions, and a few days later reported that, on the receipt of reliable information about the Roman army, all the Suebi had retired, with the whole of their force and those which they had raised from their allies, to the farthest extremity of their country, where there was an immense forest called Bacenis, stretching far into the interior and forming a natural barrier between the Suebi and the Cherusci, which prevented them from raiding and damaging each other's territory. On the edge of this forest, they said, the Suebi had resolved to await the arrival of the Romans." (Caesar, *Commentarii de Bello Gallico*, VI, 10).

This turn of events put Caesar and the Romans in a very precarious situation, leaving the Romans to determine whether they should pursue the Suebi into the forest, stay near the Rhine, or retreat back to Gaul. Caesar knew that following the Suebi into the forest was probably a death trap. He did not know the size of the Suebi forces, how big the forest was, or even what type of terrain may be there beyond the initial trees. Most importantly, he did not know if there were enough resources to support his army. He explained, "Learning from the scouts of the Ubii that the Suebi had retired into the forests, Caesar was afraid that if he followed them he might run short of corn, since, as already said, none of the Germans pay much attention to agriculture. He therefore decided to advance no farther. However, so as not to let the natives think they had seen the last of him, he left the greater part of the bridge standing. In order to hold up any reinforcements which they might try to send to Gaul, after withdrawing his army, he broke down the end that touched the Ubian bank for a distance of two hundred feet, and, at the Gallic end, erected a four-storeyed tower, posted a detachment of twelve cohorts to protect the bridge and fortified the position with strong defence works." (Caesar, *Commentarii de Bello Gallico*, VI, 29).

The construction of the tower marked the end of Caesar's involvement in Germania and with the Suebi, although the Romans and the Suebi would later have several meaningful interactions.

Early Suebi Culture

Due to problems with chronology, nomenclature, and primary source material, reconstructing early Suebi culture is difficult. Since the Suebi were not literate until much later (when they became known as the Sueves and ruled over what is today Portugal), there are no Suebi sources from their early history. And because of that, modern scholars also have to rely on archaeology to date their early movements and chronology. Finally, there is the problem of differentiating the early Suebi from the other Germanic tribes they lived alongside. Unfortunately, many of the details of early Suebi culture will probably remain forever a mystery, but Caesar and Tacitus offer glimpses into Germanic culture generally and Suebi culture specifically.

Although Caesar and Tacitus were separated by more than a century, their observations of the Germans were very similar and consistent. A lot had changed during that time in Rome, but for the people of Germania, life had continued much as it always had. According to Caesar, one of the most intriguing aspects of Suebi culture (and perhaps one of the most detestable in his eyes) was their communal way of life. He wrote, "Those who are left at home have to support the men in the army, as well as themselves, and the next year take their turn of service, while the others stay at home. Thus both agriculture, and military instruction and training, continue without interruption. No land, however, is the private property of private individuals, and no one is allowed to cultivate the same plot for more than one year." (Caesar, *Commentarii de Bello Gallico*, IV, 1).

All of this was very much antithetical to the Romans, especially a patrician such as Caesar who was accustomed to a very defined, regimented social caste system. Caesar continued by adding that the Suebi essentially practiced a sort of tariff system whereby imported goods were greatly restricted, with the sole exception of horses. In fact, Caesar claimed they only allowed non-Suebi merchants into their lands to sell goods of Suebi origin, writing, "Traders are admitted into their country more because they want to sell their booty than because they stand in any need of imports. Even horses, which the Gauls are inordinately fond of and purchase at big prices, are not imported by the Germans. They are content with their home-bred horses, which, although undersized and ugly, are rendered capable of very hard work by daily exercise." (Caesar, *Commentarii de Bello Gallico*, IV, 2).

This would also have been something that Romans of all backgrounds opposed. All Romans, patrician and plebian, believed in a relatively free market, where even poor Romans had the ability to make a profit.

While Caesar and the Romans may have looked down upon the structure of Suebi society and their economy, there were elements of Suebi culture they respected. The Romans tended to view different people much as they did animals, with certain "breeds" being admired for their beauty and abilities more than others. They generally admired the Germans for their good looks, martial abilities, and overall virility. Caesar seemed particularly impressed with the Suebi's lifestyle, writing, "They do not eat much cereal food, but live chiefly on milk and meat, and spend much time in hunting. Their diet, daily exercise, and the freedom from restraint that they enjoy – for from childhood they do not know what compulsion or discipline is, and do nothing against their inclination – combine to make them strong and as tall as giants. They inure themselves, in spite of the very cold climate in which they live, to wear no clothing but skins – and these so scanty that a large part of the body is uncovered – and to bathe in the rivers." (Caesar, *Commentarii de Bello Gallico*, IV, I).

Tacitus bolstered this assessment by noting that they rarely intermarried with other groups: "For myself, I concur in opinion with such as suppose the people of Germany never to have mingled by inter-marriages with other nations, but to have remained a people pure, and independent, and resembling none but themselves. Hence amongst such a mighty multitude of men, the same make and form is found in all, eyes stern and blue, yellow hair, huge bodies, but vigorous only in the first onset. Of pains and labour they are not equally patient, nor can they at all endure thrift and heat. To bear hunger and cold they are hardened by their climate and soil." (Tacitus, *Germania*, I).

Both descriptions are fairly consistent, with Tacitus focusing a bit more on the people's physical description. It is interesting that although Caesar believed the Suebi generally surrendered to their pleasures, which would be frowned upon in Roman society, the result was that they grew to be physically strong.

Tacitus was obviously interested in the physical appearance of the German people, but much more of his work on the Suebi and their neighbors was dedicated to their religion. The ancient Germans followed a polytheistic system that was in many ways similar to what the Norse still practiced hundreds of years later. Deities of war, harvest, and fertility were among the most important, with Tacitus and other Romans recognizing using the names of their own Roman deities to describe them: "Of all the Gods, Mercury is he whom they worship most. To him on certain stated days it is lawful to offer even human victims. Hercules and Mars they appease with beasts usually allowed for sacrifice. Some of the Suevians make likewise immolations to Isis. Concerning the cause and original of this foreign sacrifice, I have found small light; unless the figure of her image formed like a ialley, show that such devotion arrived from abroad. For the rest, from the grandeur and majesty of beings celestial, they judge it altogether unsuitable to hold the Gods enclosed within walls, or to represent them under any human likeness. They consecrate whole woods and groves, and by the names of the Gods they call these recesses; divinities these, which only in contemplation and mental reverence they behold." (Tacitus, *Germania*, I).

Mercury was probably the equivalent of Thor, Mars was probably the Germanic war god Tyr, and Isis was likely equated with the Germanic fertility and beauty goddess. The manner in which Tacitus describes how the Suebi worshipped their gods in the outdoors also coincides with the practices of contemporary and later Germanic groups, as well as their Celtic contemporaries on the other side of the Rhine River.

Tacitus also described the style of clothing and other cultural details of the German people. He noted that many of these people adopted manners like the Suebi, while being somehow distinct from them: "Nor less powerful are the several people beyond them; namely, the

Marsignians, the Gothinians, the Osians and the Burians, who altogether enclose the Marcomanians and Quadians behind. Of those, the Marsignians and the Burians in speech and dress resemble the Suevians. From the Gallic language spoken by the Gothinians, and from that of Pannonia by the Osians, it is manifest that neither of these people are Germans; as it is also from their bearing to pay tribute. Upon them as upon aliens their tribute is imposed, partly by the Sarmatians, partly by the Quadians." (Tacitus, *Germania*, II).

The passage does seem to confirm Caesar's claim that the Suebi were a large and influential tribe. It should be pointed out, though, that neither Caesar nor Tacitus spent any considerable time among the Suebi, so much of what they wrote about them was based on the generalities of the region and people who inhabited it.

Another thing to keep in mind is that the style of historical writing and geography that Caesar and Tacitus practiced was the classical model that began with the Greeks, whereby non-Greek or non-Roman people were generally depicted as wholly foreign and usually inferior. Some people who came before the Greeks and Romans, such as the Egyptians and Mesopotamians, were given special status, but all the other people of the world were variously lumped together and depicted as *topos*. For example, the Scythians played an important role in the works of the Greek historians as the "others" living on the fringes of civilization and always a threat. In Caesar's work, the Suebi and some other Germanic tribes fill this role (Krebs 2006, 122). Despite giving the Suebi Scythian characteristics, they, along with their neighbors living to the north and west of the Rhine, were depicted as freer than the more civilized Celts and Germans of Gaul (Schadee 2008, 163). In essence, the Romans' descriptions of the Suebi could have been applicable to the other Germanic tribes living on the north and east sides of the Rhine because the concept was what was most important to the Romans (Brown 2014, 397).

The Roman *topos* of the Suebi people was also extended to their land to a certain extent. For the Romans, foreign topography was almost as alluring as foreign people. Vast deserts, rainforests, and sizable temperate forests were not common sites for the urban dwelling Romans, so when they encountered new people to conquer, their lands also had to be considered. When the Romans first invaded Gaul, they faced hostile people and hostile forests, which they eventually conquered, but the vastness of Germania's forests seemed to be unconquerable (Krebs 2006, 123). The geography and the Suebi's semi-nomadic nature ensured they could never be precisely located and therefore never truly conquered (Schadee 2008, 168).

The Suebi were mentioned during the reign of Augustus,

who came to power through a series of civil wars and oversaw the establishment of the *Pax Romana* in the beginning of the 1st century CE. While his focus was mostly on domestic concerns, the non-Romans living on the edges of the empire continued to challenge Roman authority, and once more the name of the Suebi was mentioned as a problematic Germanic tribe. The Roman historian Suetonius (69-122 CE) explained, "Either as a local commander or as commander-in-chief at Rome, Augustus conquered Cantabria, Aquitania, Pannonia, Dlamatia and the whole of Illyricum, besides Raetia and the Alpine tribes known as the Vindelici and Salassi. He also checked the raids of the Dacians, inflicting heavy casualties on them – three of their generals fell in action; drove all the Germans back across the Elbe, except the Suebi and Sigambri, who surrendered and agreed to settle in Gallic territory near the Rhine; and pacified other tribes who gave trouble." (Suetonius, *The Twelve Caesars*, Divus Augustus, 20).

It should be noted that this was only a portion of the Suebi that settled in Gaul, and likely only a very small number. The remainder stayed in Germania, which is where they were living when Tacitus wrote about them. For the next several centuries, the Suebi would blend into their surroundings and not be heard from until the collapse of Rome took place in the late 5th century and the great wave of migrations inundated Europe.

The Sueves

In the centuries after Caesar and Tacitus wrote about the Suebi, the Romans focused most of their resources on maintaining the empire they had built. Gaul became a Romanized province, and so too did Britain, but Germania was left alone after the Varus and three legions were ambushed and entirely massacred in the Teutoburg Forest in 9 CE (Grant 1994, 57). The Romans dealt more with the Persians and people on their eastern border in the 1st and 2nd centuries CE, before the tribes of Germania began pushing across the border into the empire, at first gradually and then as a torrent, beginning in the 3rd century. The Visigoths were the first significant tribe to raid and occupy Roman territory in the late 4th century, and they were then followed by several more tribes. Part of the Suebi would be part of this early, violent wave of migration.

The migrations that took place in Europe during this period – sometimes referred to by historians as the "Great Migrations" or "Germanic Migrations" – came about due to several factors. Population increases in Germania certainly played a role, pushing some tribes or individuals closer to the Rhine and Danube. The migrations of non-Germanic tribes like the Huns also created a "domino effect" of stronger and larger tribes pushing the weaker tribes farther west and south (Jotischky and Hull 2005, 20). These pressures on the Suebi were likely the same as they were throughout Germania, and by the 5th century, the Asiatic Huns added more pressure to the tribes of Germania (James 2001, 62). It is almost certain that the arrival of the Huns proved to be the final straw in the camel's back when it came to compelling Suebi leave their homeland.

One important factor was the allure of Rome itself. The Romans and the "barbarians," as the Romans referred to them, had a love-hate relationship. The Germanic tribes saw the Romans as both an enemy and worthy of adoration. The Germans respected Roman civilization and order, and they coveted Roman wealth. The Germanic tribes that began migrating into Roman territory did so to raid for booty, but also to become Roman citizens. The pressure the Germanic tribes exerted on the empire was intense, and when combined with the social and economic problems Rome had been experiencing for centuries, the emperors made the momentous decision to oversee a controlled withdrawal of certain territories.

In 406, the Romans withdrew from most of Gaul and left the Rhine River barrier wide open. It was almost immediately crossed by a number of tribes (Bury 1967, 81). The Suebi, or part of them, crossed the Rhine with the Germanic Vandals and the non-Germanic Alans. The fact that the Suebi suddenly reentered the historical record after such a long absence is important, but the identity of the Suebi can be a bit confusing in the subsequent medieval texts if not considered with the Roman texts. The 6th century monk Gregory of Tours wrote that in addition to joining the Vandals on the migration across the Rhine, the Suebi became known by other names: "The Suebi, also called the Alamanni, followed the Vandals, and seized Galicia." (Gregory of Tours, *The History of the Franks*, II, 2). This confusion is compounded by the fact that the Suebi were later known as the Sueves after they arrived in Hispania.

The changing names may be linked to the nature of the Suebi's society or societies. As noted earlier by Tacitus, the Suebi were probably more of a confederacy or coalition than one single tribe. Even earlier, Caesar noted how other Germanic tribes lived under the Suebi, whom he considered the most powerful of all the people in Germania. It is likely that by the 5th century, the Suebi who crossed the Rhine did so in multiple waves and comprised different sub-tribes. The main host of Suebi, who became the Sueves, took a more central route through Gaul into Hispania, while the Alamanni sub-tribe invaded and settled in southern Gaul (Jotischky and Hull 2005, 20). According to Gregory of Tours, the crossing of the Rhine conducted by the Alamanni and Suebi was led by a king known as Chroc: "At the same time, Chroc, King of the Alamanni, assembled an army and invaded Gaul. There is said to have been no limit to this Chroc's overweening pride. He was the perpetrator of a long series of crimes, being under the influence, so they say, of his wicked mother, and now, as I have told you, he mobilized the people of the Alamanni, invaded the whole of Gaul, and destroyed down to its very foundations every single building which had been put up in ancient times." (Gregory of Tours, *The History of the Franks,* I, 32).

This account likely conflated the main host of the Suebi with the Alamanni sub-tribe, because as noted above, the latter's invasion of Gaul was more limited in nature. Either way, this invasion of Gaul was devastating, forcing the Romano-Gauls to move their capital to Arles (James 2001, 64). It also paved the way for another Germanic tribe, the Franks, to conquer the entire province.

Neither the Suebi nor their Vandal and Alan allies apparently had any intention of staying in Gaul. After pillaging many of the province's towns and committing a fair amount of atrocities against the churches there, the three tribes continued their journey across the Pyrenees into modern Spain. Hispania was still technically a Roman province in the early 5th century, but as with Gaul and Britain, the Romans were forced to remove most of their defenders. The Suebi, who became known as the Sueves at that point, eventually began fighting with their once allies, as well as the Visigoths who were already in the region. The situation became very confusing and complex, and the history of the region is hard to make out due to the lack of available primary sources (Halsall 2007, 226).

The Visigoths were not able to fend off the new invaders and left Spain in 418, although they would later return with a vengeance. This meant that the Sueves, Alans, and Vandals could divide Hispania among themselves and establish new political dynasties. The Sueve Dynasty began with King Hermerich, who ruled from 409-438, establishing the foundations of the Sueve kingdom and the modern state of Portugal.

Building this kingdom would not be easy, though, as the Sueves immediately faced several obstacles. The alliance between the Vandals, Sueves, and Alans quickly became undone once they settled in Spain and there was nothing left to conquer. The Sueves found themselves fighting with the junior partner in their alliance, the Alans, in 418. The war with the Alans was inconclusive, but it pushed the Sueves into the region of Gallaecia, which is roughly equivalent with northwest Portugal (Fontes and Seidel 2014, 32). The migration was purely defensive on the part of the Sueves, at least initially, but it ultimately proved to be beneficial for them as a people.

Once the conflict with the Alans subsided, the Sueves faced an even bigger threat from the Vandals. King Gunderic of the Hasding branch of the Vandals turned on Hermerich and the Sueves, driving them into the mountains of what is today Portugal (Halsall 2007, 233). The Sueves were all but finished when the Romans came to their rescue in 420 (Halsall 2007, 233). The Roman general Constantius, who would rule as Emperor Constantius III for a few months in 421, was given the challenging and unenviable task of restoring order and the Romans' hold over Spain. Since Constantius did not have the manpower to do so directly, he was forced to play the Machiavellian game of pitting one side against the other, while never letting any of the tribes get too powerful.

Constantius' involvement gave the Sueves some breathing room, but their quest to establish a kingdom in Iberia was not yet over. As the reigns of the Roman emperors got shorter and shorter in the 5th century, the generals were given a freer hand to develop political and military policy in the outlying provinces. The Roman general Flavius Aetius (391-454) became the single most effective person to challenge the barbarians, doing so through a combination of superb military strategy and political posturing among the barbarian tribes. In Spain, Aetius recognized that the Vandals were the biggest threat to the Roman establishment, so he made an alliance with the Sueves. The Vandals realized that their kingdom in Spain would always be threatened, so they decided to migrate one final time to North Africa. As the Vandals were leaving Spain in 427 and 429, though, they attacked and defeated the Sueve-Roman alliance, which had long-lasting repercussions on the Iberian Peninsula (Halsall 2007, 240).

  Despite losing on the battlefield to the Vandals, the defeats were actually blessings in disguise for the nascent Sueve kingdom. The Vandals and their Alan allies completely left Iberia after 429, and at the same time they had eliminated the threat of the Roman presence in the area as well. This situation left the Sueves free to further consolidate Gallaecia as their home, look to the south for future expansion, and make another deal with Aetius that would make them the sole German federation in the region.

  When Rechila (r. 438-448) became the king of the Sueves, he inherited a kingdom that included Gallaecia and had the rest of the Iberian Peninsula open to his advances. The Romans still technically controlled Hispania, but they were reliant upon their Germanic allies to keep order, so with the Vandals, Alans, and Visigoths gone, Rechila was free to conquer most of the western slice of the peninsula. Like nearly all the Germanic tribes that preceded them in Europe, the Sueves were willing to get what they could from the Romans and then turn on them if need be. The Sueves raided Seville, Baetica, and Carthaginiensis among other locations in Roman-held Hispania (Fontes and Seidel 2014, 32). Thus, by the mid-5th century, the Sueves had established a powerful kingdom on the Atlantic coast of Hispania and influenced most of the peninsula, which quickly brought the attention of others in the region.

In 445, the Vandals ruled a kingdom based in what is today Tunisia that included Sicily and most of the other islands in the eastern Mediterranean. With that, the Vandals had built a sedentary kingdom, but they did not exactly become sedentary people. They continued to raid throughout North Africa and southern Europe, and in 445 the Vandals raided the Gallaecian coastline. Some modern scholars believe that the reason for this Vandal attack on Sueve land was instigated by the Romans, who were desperate to check the Sueves' growing power in southwestern Europe (Halsall 2007, 249-50). It may also be simply that the Sueves' kingdom was relatively close to the Vandals, so it proved to be an easy target. Another reason could be that the Vandals believed they had unfinished business with the Sueves. Whatever the reasons, the attacks did not have any major effect on the Sueves' kingdom, as Rechila was able to pass the throne relatively unaffected to Rechiar (ruled 448-456).

Rechiar's reign represents the last in the early line of stable Sueve rulers in Iberia. Rechiar continued raids and military campaigns throughout Iberia, particularly into the Ebro Valley to Zaragoza, and later as far as the Pyrenees (Halsall 2007, 250). Rechiar also made other political moves to stabilize his kingdom. Rechiar married the Visigoth King Theodoric's daughter in Gaul, thereby tying him closer to the Goths and the Romans (Halsall 2007, 250). The Visigoths were then the most loyal of all the Romans' German allies, even though they had previously caused severe destruction in Roman territories. The Visigoths controlled a large part of southern Gaul to the Pyrenees, with the Franks to their north and the Romans and Sueves to their south. The diplomatic marriage went well for Rechiar and the Sueves at first, as it integrated them further into the Roman-Germanic culture that was developing in Western Europe. The Sueves began converting to Arian Christianity at that time, a requirement for Rechiar to marry Theodoric's daughter, although most of the people retained their Germanic pagan beliefs.

Rechiar also pursued deeper diplomatic relations with the Romans, signing a peace treaty with Mansuetus, the Roman count of Spain, in 456 (Halsall 2007, 254-5). The peace treaty with Rome and the diplomatic marriage to Theodoric's daughter would have seemingly placated

Rechiar and the Sueves, placing them into the status of "former barbarians" such as the Visigoths, but apparently the warrior spirit was still strong in the Sueve kingdom. Rechiar continued to attack Roman territory in an effort to conquer all of Iberia for the Sueves. Rome was on the verge of collapsing in 456, but the Visigoths had become the major power in Western Europe and were increasingly looking south of the Pyrenees to expand their possessions. When Rechiar broke the treaty he had only recently signed with the Romans, the Romans called on the Visigoths, who allied with the Germanic Burgundians to invade Spain. A Visigoth-Burgundian army, led by Rechiar's brother-in-law, Theodoric II, defeated Rechiar and the Sueves on October 5, 456 near the city of Astorga. The result was disastrous for the king, who was executed by his brother-in-law, and the Sueves, who descended into a period of anarchy (Halsall 2007, 260).

After Rechiar was killed, the Sueve kingdom was ruled by a succession of short-lived and often weak kings. Civil strife and conflict within the Sueve royal family also plagued the dynasty during this period. For example, from 460-464, two men named Rechimund and Frumar both claimed the throne, which demonstrated the instability within the kingdom (Fontes and Seidel 2014, 34). Continued threats from the Vandals on the coastline and the Visigoths to the north also threatened to destroy the

Sueves, even as they continued to integrate into the Western European cultural fabric.

During Europe's transition from the Roman Empire to the Early Middle Ages, early Church historians often focused their writings on one barbarian tribe or a specific geographic region. For example, Bede primarily wrote about the Angles, Saxons, and Jutes, while Gregory of Tours focused on the Franks. The primary chronicler of the Sueves was the 5th century bishop Hydatis, who lived in and served the region of Gallaecia. It is believed that Hydatis died in 468 or shortly thereafter, as that is when his history ends (Halsall 2007, 300). Unfortunately, that is also where the written accounts of the Iberian Suebi kingdom also end, so historians are forced to rely on archaeology and the mentions of the Sueves in other histories to reconstruct the chronology of the last years of the Iberian Suebi kingdom as much as possible.

Modern studies have determined that although the Sueves converted to Arian Christianity like the Visigoths, Vandals, and most other Germanic tribes, they joined the Roman Catholic Church during the 560s. The conversion took place either during the rule of Ariamir (r. 558-561 or 566) or Theodmir (r. 561 or 566-570) (Fontes and Seidel 2014, 34). The move towards the Roman Catholic Church was probably a cynical ploy by the nobility more than anything, as the Catholics' power was growing during the period. Although the last Western Roman emperor abdicated the throne in 476, Rome continued to be culturally important and eventually became the seat of the Catholic Church. Eventually, all the Germanic tribes converted from Arianism to Roman Catholicism, so the Iberian Suebi leaders probably thought it was politically expedient to follow suit.

That said, if the move towards Catholicism was political in nature, it ultimately failed. The Sueves grew weaker while the Visigoths grew stronger and eventually conquered the entire Iberian Peninsula. The last Suebian king in Portugal was Malarich, who died in 585 after less than one year of rule (Fontes and Seidel 2014, 33). The Suebian legacy can still be seen today in Portugal in certain place names, but few other elements of the Sueves' nearly 200 years of rule in the region can be found.

The Remaining Suebi in France and Germany

As the Suebi ravaged Gaul and established a kingdom in Portugal, other sub-tribes of the people stayed in Germania or made less penetrating forays into Gaul and other locations. These Suebi are the ancestors of many people in Europe, and they often built some of medieval Europe's earliest kingdoms. Like the Suebi who established a kingdom in Portugal, the Alamanni-Suebi and other Suebi sub-tribes entered the historical record as migratory marauders but eventually integrated into the many principalities and kingdoms of the era.

According to Gregory of Tours, the Alamanni-Suebi created plenty of problems for the Frankish King Childeric (r. 440-481) and the German-Italian King Odovacar (r. 476-493), just as the Saxons were also raiding parts of Gaul. Gregory of Tours wrote, "While these things were happening, a great war was waged between the Saxons and the Romans. The Saxons fled and many of their men were cut down by the Romans who pursued them. Their islands were captured and laid waste by the Franks, and many people were killed. In the ninth month of that year there was an earthquake. Odovacar made a treaty with Childeric and together they subdued the Alamanni, who had invaded a part of Italy." (Gregory of Tours, *The History of the Franks*, II, 19).

Once the Saxons were defeated, Childeric could focus his attention on subduing southern Gaul and the Alamanni-Suebi, but they proved to be a much more formidable foe. He was not able to defeat them, so the task was left to his successor, Clovis (r. 481-511). Clovis, who is often viewed as the greatest king of the Merovingian dynasty, eventually dealt with the Alamanni-Suebi decisively.

The future of the Merovingian-Frankish kingdom before Clovis came to power was questionable. The Visigoths controlled most of southern Gaul, and to the south of them were the Sueves and the remnants of the Romans. The Saxons were a constant threat from the north, coming across the Rhine River to raid as far south as Orleans, while the Alamanni-Suebi continued to be a problem south of Trier to the Loire River (Jotischky and Hull 2005, 20). Clovis would eventually become known as the greatest king of his dynasty through a combination of his success on the battlefield and his patronage of the Catholic Church. Both of these policies came together when he found himself on the battlefield against the Alamanni-Suebi, and Gregory of Tours claimed he was helped by divine intervention: "Finally, war broke out against the Alamanni and in this conflict he was forced by necessity to accept what he had refused of his own free will. It so turned out that when the two armies met on the battlefield there was great slaughter and the troops of Clovis were rapidly being annihilated. He raised his eyes to heaven when he saw this, felt compunction in his heart and was moved to tears. 'Jesus Christ,' he said . . . 'I will be baptized in your name. I have called upon my own gods, but, as I see only too clearly, they have no intention of helping me.' Even as he said this, the Alamanni turned their backs and began to run away." (Gregory of Tours, *The History of the Franks*, II, 30).

By the time Clovis died in 511, he had expanded the borders of the Frankish kingdom to include most of what is today France, with the exception of the region around Dijon, which was still controlled by the Burgundians. The Alamanni-Suebi had been defeated as well between 496 and 502, though many stayed in the region and integrated themselves into Frankish culture (Kinder and Hilgemann 1974, 120-1).

By the 6th century, the Suebi had all but been integrated into the various kingdoms where they ended their migrations (Portugal, Spain, and France), but a number remained in and around their ancient homeland in what is today southern Germany. One of the last significant historical mentions of the Suebi was related to how Clovis's son and successor, Clothar I (r. 511-561) resettled many of them. This time the Suebi were referred to as "Swabians," and they were moved to lands formerly held by the Saxons. The Saxons responded with force, but they were utterly defeated by the Swabians. Gregory of Tours wrote, "When Alboin went off to Italy, Clothar I and Sigibert settled the Swabians and other peoples in the territory which he had left vacant. . . The Saxons who were furious with the Swabians because they themselves had previously held all the land, showed no inclination whatsoever to make peace. Then the Swabians offered half, and afterwards two thirds, keeping only one third for themselves. The Saxons still refused, and the Swabians then offered not only two thirds of the land, but all the flocks and herds on it, if only the Saxons would refrain from war. The Saxons would not accept even this offer, for they were determined to do battle. . . The battle was joined, but out of twenty-six thousand Saxons who took part, no fewer than twenty thousand were slain. There were only six thousand Swabians, and four hundred and eighty of them were killed, those who remained alive winning the victory." (Gregory of Tours, *The History of the Franks,* V, 15).

After that, the term Swabian was used for "Suebi" and "Sueves" in nearly every historical text. Over 2,000 years after they arrived, the region in southern Germany known as Swabia can trace its linguistic and cultural origins to the Suebi, even as the memory of those origins were all but forgotten by the end of the Middle Ages.

Online Resources

<u>Other books about ancient history by Charles River Editors</u>

Further Reading

Brown, Robert D. 2014. "A Civilized Gaul: Caesar's Portrait of Piso Aquitanus ('De Bello Gallico' 4.12.4-6)." *Mnemosyne* 67: 391-404.

Bury, J.B. 1967. *The Invasion of Europe by the Barbarians*. New York: W.W. Norton.

Chadwick, Henry. 2001. "Evoi: On Taking Leave of Antiquity." In *The Oxford History of the Roman World*, edited by John Boardman, Jasper Griffin, and Oswyn Murray, 449-478. Oxford: Oxford University Press.

Dunn, Geoffrey D. 2015. "Flavius Constantius, Galla Placidia, and the Aquitanian Settlement ofthe Goths." *Phoenix* 69: 376-393.

Fontes, Luis, and Ute Seidel. 2014. "Das Suebische Königrech auf der Iberischen Halbinsel." *Archäologie in Deutschland* 5: 32-35.

Goffart, Walter. 2006. *Barbarian Tides: The Migration Age and the Later Roman Empire*. Philadelphia: University of Pennsylvania Press.

Grant, Michacl. 1994. *Atlas of Classical History*. 5th cd. New York: Oxford University Press.

Gregory of Tours. 1974. *The History of the Franks*. Translated by Lewis Thorpe. London: Penguin.

Halsall, Guy. 2007. *Barbarian Migrations and the Roman West, 376-568*. Cambridge: Cambridge University Press.

James, Edward. 2001. "The Northern World in the Dark

Ages, 400-900." In *The Oxford History of Medieval Europe*, ed. George Holmes, 59-108. Oxford: Oxford University Press.

Jotischky, Andrew and Caroline Hall. 2005. *The Penguin Historical Atlas of the Medieval World*. London: Penguin Books.

Julius Caesar. 1982. *Commentarii de Bello Gallico*. Translated by S. A. Handford. Revised with a New Introduction by Jane F. Gardner. London: Penguin.

Kinder, Herman, and Werner Hilgemann. 1974. *The Anchor Atlas of World History*. Vol. 1, *From the Stone Age to the Eve of the French Revolution*. Translated by Ernest A. Menze. Mapsby Harald and Ruth Bukor. Garden City, New York: Anchor Books.

Krebs, Cristopher B. 2006. "'Imaginary Geography' In Caesar's *Belleum Gallicum*." *American Journal of Philology* 127: 111-136.

Schadee, Hester. 2008. "Caesar's Construction of Northern Europe: Inquiry, Contact and Corruption in 'De Bello Gallico.'" *Classical Quarterly* 58: 158-180.

Suetonius. 2007. *The Twelve Caesars*. Translated by Robert Graves. London: Penguin.

Tacitus. 2021. *Germania*. Translated by Thomas

Gordon. Internet Source

Boo.https://sourcebooks.fordham.edu/basis/tacitus-germanygord.asp.

Free Books by Charles River Editors

We have brand new titles available for free most days of the week. To see which of our titles are currently free, click on this link.

Discounted Books by Charles River Editors

We have titles at a discount price of just 99 cents everyday. To see which of our titles are currently 99 cents, click on this link.